# I AM ONE

Written by L.D. Keeys

Illustrated by M. Octavius Keeys

Balboa Press books may be ordered through booksellers or by contacting:

Balboa Press
A Division of Hay House
1663 Liberty Drive
Bloomington, IN 47403
www.balboapress.com
1 (877) 407-4847

Interior Graphics/Art Credit: Mark O. Keeys

ISBN: 978-1-9822-1550-7 (sc)
ISBN: 978-1-9822-1549-1 (e)

Library of Congress Control Number: 2018913186

Print information available on the last page.

Balboa Press rev. date: 11/29/2018

BALBOA.
PRESS
A DIVISION OF HAY HOUSE

# Table of Contents

# A Message to Parents and Teachers

When I first heard of the Law of Attraction, I felt a deep resonance within. Always a seeker of universal truth, I believe that this awareness appeared in my life at the exact moment that I was ready to receive it. Knowing the common adage, "believe, achieve and receive," I understood the law intuitively. I also recalled Matthew 7:7, "Ask and it will be given to you; seek and you will find." These principles are deeply rooted in American colloquial speech. Yet, in our complex world, we are challenged to believe that concepts as simple as these are our birthright.

We are connected to a divine power that expresses itself though love and laws. These laws are always working regardless of our awareness or acceptance of them. When we are mindful of these laws along with our thoughts, feelings and beliefs, we activate the unlimited powers, resources and gifts of the Universe.

Spiritual laws have the same significance as physical laws. Our spiritual masters have taught these laws throughout time, in myriad ways, in countless languages and innumerable cultures. The Bible, the Torah, the Quran, The Principles of Maat, the Bhagavad Gita, the Tao Te Ching, and volumes of poetry and philosophy acknowledge the existence of these laws.

Throughout the years as a student of universal spiritual laws, it occurred to me that if children were taught that religious principles were founded on spiritual laws that function with the same efficacy as physical laws, i.e., the law of gravity, that the recognition and utilization of these laws could become routine. Children could develop a habitual practice of expecting and manifesting their highest potential.

Formerly enslaved African and abolitionist, Frederick Douglass emphasized that "it is easier to build strong children than to repair broken men." As an introduction to universal spiritual laws (all laws are not included in this volume), **I AM ONE** aims to contribute to the fortifying of holistically strong children, who will eventually grow to be holistically strong adults.

There are many universal spiritual laws. However, all laws extend from the Law of One. Everything in the Universe is connected. Romans 8:28 asserts, "All things work together for good. . ." This truth is the foundation for metaphysical understanding.

Although **I AM ONE** is a children's book, it is to be read and enjoyed by both children and adults. Read this book with your children, review the appendix and recite the affirmations with a loving heart and an open mind. In this era of human evolution, **I AM ONE** is a transformative message for the awakening of enlightened souls.

—L.D. Keeys

# Dedication

I dedicate this book to my husband, M. Octavius Keeys, who is both my illustrator and my muse. He is my best demonstration of The Law of Attraction. As I mindfully resonated love, he appeared. Together we grow more deeply in love and in our understanding of the laws of God.

I also dedicate this book to my mother, Hazel Dozier Dunbar. Her love and devotion exist in the essence of my being. My gratitude is most profoundly expressed as I extend to the world the love that she gave to me.

## —L.D. Keeys

I dedicate this book to L.D. Keeys, my wife and best friend whose chosen life path synchronizes and harmonizes with mine. I also dedicate this book to Mia, Marcia, Mark, Jr., Calvin and Kadie Keeys, our daughters and sons whose presence has been and continues to be school for my soul.

Finally, I dedicate this book to my father and mother, Calvin and Lucille Keeys. They laid a solid foundation for me to build upon and continually grow.

## —M. Octavius Keeys

# I AM ONE

Written by L.D. Keeys
Illustrated by M. Octavius Keeys

I am grateful

I am one with the Law of Gratitude

Knowing that the Universe is bountiful

I give thanks for its magnitude

I am generous
I am one with the Law of Flow
All good gifts surround us
I release and let things go

I am graceful

GOD surrounds me in grace

I am intentionally mindful

of GOD's divine embrace

I am wealthy

I am one with the Law of Abundance

I am wise, happy and healthy

The whole Universe is my substance

I am magnetic
I attract what I believe
My thoughts are prophetic
I create what I perceive

10

11

I am brilliance

I am one with the Law of Success

I am Universal intelligence

I am a creative genius

13

I am prosperous
I am one with the Law of Prosperity
My riches are innumerous
My blessings are my charity

14

15

I am pure

I am one with the Law of Purity

The love of God protects me for sure.

My faith is my security

I am forgiving

I am one with the Law of Forgiveness

I let go of the past to serve the living

and activate Christ Consciousness

18

I am confident

I am one with the Law of Decree

In my mind I hold the equivalent

I manifest what I can see

21

I am whole

I am one with the Law of Healing

I am perfect in body, spirit and soul

My health reveals my feelings

23

I am limitless
I embody the Law of One
I know that GOD is all there is
So, let GOD's will be done

# THE END

26

# The Law of Gratitude

**Gratitude** | noun | The quality or feeling of being grateful or thankful.

We know that we are aligned with the Law of Gratitude when we are mindfully grateful of the infinite blessings that we receive every day. Psalm 107:1 affirms, "Give thanks to the Lord for He is good! His loving-kindness lasts forever." As we remain in a state of gratefulness, knowing and believing that we already have all that is required to live our best lives, blessings flow with amazing abundance.

To remain in a state of gratefulness, we can keep a gratitude journal. Each day, we can record at least three persons, things or circumstances for which we are grateful. We can acknowledge our gratitude with a simple prayer – Thank you God!

**Affirmation:** *I am deeply grateful for the blessings that flow from the magnificent abundance and endless generosity of the Universe. I live in a state of gratitude for all that I have.*

# The Law of Circulation (Flow)

**Circulation** | noun | An act or instance of circulating, moving in a circle or circuit, or flowing.

The Law of Circulation challenges us to let go of anything that no longer serves a purpose. Circulation involves a consistent flow of energy. When we hold onto items, clothing, circumstances, etc. that no longer serve a purpose, we block new, unlimited possibilities from entering into our lives.

Luke 6:38 asserts, "Give and it shall be given unto you." We know that we are aligned with the Law of Circulation when we give generously; easily letting go of items, clothing, circumstances, etc. that have outlived their usefulness, offering those possessions that we continue to love that could potentially assist the growth and development of another, and providing, from our overflow, that which serves humanity. Then, we must trust that whatever we require to live our best lives is available and flowing freely.

**Affirmation:** *I release that which is no longer useful to me in order to make space for that which I require to live my best life.*

**Grace** | noun | A manifestation of favor, especially by a superior [Supreme Being].

The Law of Grace imparts favor, forgiveness and empathy into our lives. Because our thoughts create our circumstances, we know that we are aligned with the Law of Grace when our thoughts, feelings, beliefs and actions are aligned with the unconditional love of the Universe.

John 1:16 upholds, "And from God's fullness we have all received, grace upon grace." Grace is a miracle worker that has the power to transform the world.  In order to remain in a state of grace, we must be loving, empathetic and forgiving to everyone, including ourselves, everywhere and all the time.

**Affirmation:** *I unconditionally give and receive love, forgiveness and empathy. I am surrounded by the grace of God.*

# The Law of Abundance

**Abundance** | noun | An extremely plentiful or over-sufficient quantity or supply.

As with all universal spiritual laws, the Law of Abundance is always available to us. To the degree that we believe, we have access to all that exists in the Universe. Our abundance comes in many forms including happiness, health and wealth.

James 1:2-4 emphasizes, "Let steadfastness have its full effect, that you may be perfect and complete, and lacking in nothing." Because the Universe consistently conspires in our favor, the degree to which we are happy, healthy and wealthy is a direct reflection of our deepest thoughts, feelings and beliefs. In order to remain in a state of abundance, we must give generously while affirming that all of our needs are met. We must trust that all is available to us and that we deserve to receive it.

**Affirmation:** *The Universe is lush and overflowing with abundance. I know that I am a part of that abundance. Therefore, my life is lush and overflowing with abundance.*

**Attraction** | noun | The act or power of attracting. A person or thing that draws, attracts, allures, or entices.

The Law of Attraction affirms that we attract into our lives that which we think, feel and believe. When our thoughts, feelings and beliefs get impressed upon the Law of Attraction, the results are a direct manifestation of our deepest self. The extent to which we do not understand the circumstances and conditions that we attract into our lives reflects the extent to which we are not in touch with our own thoughts, feelings and beliefs.

Romans 12:2 proclaims, "Do not be conformed to this world, but be transformed by the renewal of your mind, that by testing you may discern what is the will of God, what is good and acceptable and perfect." In other words, to proactively utilize the Law of Attraction, we must be mindfully aware of our thoughts, feelings and beliefs. Only then will our lives be transformed.

**Affirmation:** *All that exists in the Universe is good. I am a part of that good. Therefore, all that I attract into my life is good.*

**Success** | noun | The accomplishment of an aim or purpose.

We are aligned with the Law of Success when our thoughts, feelings and beliefs resonate on the same vibrational level as our desired outcome. We must set a clear intention and work diligently and consistently towards our goals regardless of the obstacles that we may perceive along the journey.

When a seed is planted in the ground, a metamorphosis occurs in the soil that we cannot see until the plant emerges. Just as we trust that the physical laws of nature are working, we must also trust, be patient and have faith that the spiritual laws are working.

Matthew 6:33 declares, "Seek first the kingdom of God and his righteousness, and all these things will be added to you." Success requires faith in God, ourselves and the process of life. When we truly believe in ourselves and know what we want, we succeed.

**Affirmation:** *I know that God always says "yes!" I will succeed to the degree that I believe.*

**Prosperity** | noun | A successful, flourishing, or thriving condition, especially in financial respects; good fortune.

Prosperity consciousness is a deep conviction that we deserve access to the resources that exist in the Universe. We know that we are aligned with the Law of Prosperity when we witness abundance in our lives.

Philippians 4:19 states, "God will supply every need of yours according to his riches." When we believe that all of our needs are met, the Universe responds in abundance. However, money is not the only symbol of prosperity. Health, freedom, peace and access to unlimited resources are all forms of prosperity. We develop our prosperity consciousness through affirmative prayer and by giving generously.

**Affirmation:** *I know that all of my needs are met according to the riches of the God's vast Universe.*

**Purity** | noun | The condition or quality of being pure; freedom from anything that debases, contaminates, pollutes, etc.

We know that we are aligned with The Law of Purity when we emit the energy of pure love. Everything that exists in the Universe is energy vibrating at distinctive vibrational frequencies. Our thoughts, feelings and beliefs emit energy that can either have a low frequency or a high frequency. Because God is love, love vibrates at the highest frequency.

The love of God creates a barrier of protection that allows only pure, unconditional love to enter into our vibrational sphere. With this knowledge, our faith in the unconditional love of God is our best protection and security. Matthew 5:8 maintains, "Blessed are the pure in heart, for they shall see God." In other words, when we are pure in heart, we are enveloped by the unconditional love and light of God.

**Affirmation:** *I have no fear. I am shrouded and protected by the unconditional love of God.*

**Forgiveness** | noun | The action or process of forgiving or being forgiven.
**Forgive** | verb | To give up resentment of or claim to requital.

We know that we are aligned with the Law of Forgiveness when we are giving love and compassion to those whose actions have hurt us rather than holding onto pain and resentment. When we live in a state of unforgiveness, we create a barrier of bitterness that blocks our blessing from flowing.

God is pure love and does not have resentments. Because all of humanity is connected, when we hold onto resentments, we are holding offenses against ourselves. Ephesians 4:32 emphasizes, "Be kind to one another, tenderhearted, forgiving one another, as God in Christ (Consciousness) forgave you." Forgiveness is an enlightened state of consciousness.

**Affirmation:** *Love and compassion flow freely from my heart. I forgive everyone and do not hold onto pain and resentment.*

# The Law of Decree

**Decree** | noun | A formal and authoritative order, especially one having the force of law.

Through affirmative prayer, we align ourselves with the Law of Decree. When we want a circumstance to change in our lives, we must affirm the goodness that already exists in the Universe. Knowing that the Universe is good and always working to support us, we create a picture in our minds or mental equivalent of that which we desire, and watch the goodness manifest.

Mark 11:24 declares, "Therefore I tell you, whatever you ask in prayer, believe that you have received it, and it will be yours." When we set our intentions and make a decree, it is only required that we ask once. God always says "Yes." We manifest on the level of our beliefs.

**Affirmation:** *I affirm that all that I require to live my best life exists in the vastness of the Universe. I know that all goodness is mine according to the Laws of God.*

**Healing** | noun | The act or process of regaining health.

We are spiritual beings having a temporary human experience. Because we are spiritual beings, everything that we experience happens first on the spiritual level; then it manifests on the physical level in accordance with our level of consciousness. Therefore, when our bodies are out of balance, we must first determine that which we are thinking, feeling and believing that may contribute to a sense of spiritual imbalance.

We know that we are aligned with The Law of Healing when our bodies mirror the truth of who we are -- perfect, whole and complete. Proverbs 17:22 upholds, "A joyful heart is good medicine, but a crushed spirit dries up the bones." Because of this understanding, we know that our bodies do not require healing. On the spiritual level, we must affirm our health and wholeness. As we affirm the truth, our bodies follow at the level of our consciousness.

**Affirmation:** *I know that I am whole perfect and complete. My thoughts, feelings and beliefs are aligned with the consciousness of the Most High.*

**One** | adj. | Existing, acting, or considered as a single unit, entity, or individual.

The Law of One affirms that everything in the Universe is connected. Since we are energy, nothing happens in the Universe that does not eventually affect everyone everywhere. We know that we are aligned with The Law of One when we abide by Matthew 22:37. When Jesus said, "Love your neighbor as yourself," it is understood that loving our neighbor is the same as loving ourselves. We are one with God, the Universe and all that exists within it.

Genesis 1:27 states "So God created man in his own image, in the image of God he created him; male and female he created them. Each of us is made in the image and likeness of God. When we see our brothers and sisters, we see ourselves. When we embody the Law of One, we resonate on a vibrational level that sends peace and love to all of humanity. Knowing who we are is the key to transformation.

**Affirmation:** *I know that I am one with God and the Universe. As I love myself, I also love my neighbor and send the consciousness of love throughout the Universe.*

**L.D. Keeys**, M.S., M.Ed., RScP is a writer, educator, racial justice advocate and licensed spiritual life coach whose work focuses on spiritual perspectives and solutions for social issues. Possessing over twenty years of experience in higher education, she has served as an adjunct professor of sociology and African American Studies, a faculty advisor and an administrator of academic affairs. As an educational consultant, Lailah trains educators, clergy and other service professionals to develop their cultural competence.

**M. Octavius Keeys**, M.Ed., RN is an illustrator, educator, registered nurse and health and wellness practitioner. As a certified science teacher in two states, he has taught both high school and middle school. Possessing over thirty years of experience, he has given many the tools to maintain health and to provide the mind, body and soul with what is required for greater health and wellness.

Printed in the United States
By Bookmasters